DISNEY LEARNING

DISNEY·PIXAR FINDING DORY

AGES 5-6
KEY STAGE 1

Maths
Practice

Scholastic Children's Books,
Euston House,
24 Eversholt Street,
London NW1 1DB, UK

A division of Scholastic Ltd
London ~ New York ~ Toronto ~ Sydney ~ Auckland
Mexico City ~ New Delhi ~ Hong Kong

Published in the UK by Scholastic Ltd, 2016.

ISBN 978 1407 16590 5

Printed in Malaysia

2 4 6 8 10 9 7 5 3 1

Papers used by Scholastic Children's Books are made from woods grown in sustainable forests.

www.scholastic.co.uk

Welcome to the Disney Learning Programme!

Children learn best when they are having fun! The **Disney Learning Workbooks** are an engaging way for children to develop their maths skills with fun characters from the wonderful world of Disney.

The **Disney Learning Workbooks** are carefully structured to present new challenges to developing learners. Designed to support the National Curriculum in England: Mathematics Programme of Study at Key Stage 1, this title offers children the opportunity to practise skills learned at school and to consolidate their learning in a relaxed home setting with parental support. With stickers, motivating story pages and a range of maths activities related to the film *Finding Dory*, your children will have fun while improving their maths.

This book covers the core maths content that children will be taught in Year 1. Please note that schools sometimes vary the order in which maths content is taught, so you may find topics that your children haven't yet covered at school. The National Curriculum's aims are for children to develop both their understanding and fluency in maths. Fluency is when children are able to quickly recall information such as doubles or number bonds to 10 and use them efficiently.

Keep sessions short and fun. Some children may want to work independently on some of the activities while others may prefer working through the exercises with an adult. There are three 'Let's Read' stories to share, too.

Have fun with the Disney Learning programme!

Developed in conjunction with Nicola Spencer, educational consultant

Do not write in this book

Let's Practise Maths

This book is full of fun activities to help you practise key maths skills.

- Find somewhere quiet to work.

- Ask a grown-up to help you read the instructions if you are not sure what to do.

- Don't worry if you make a mistake – everyone does when they are learning! Just cross it out and try again.

You will use three important signs in this book:

+
add

–
subtract

=
equals

What is addition? +

When you count two groups or numbers to find out how many there are altogether, the answer is called the **total**. We use the **+** sign to add.

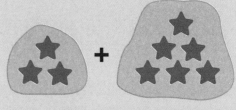

It doesn't matter in which order you add numbers, you always will get the same total.

| 3 | + | 6 | = | 9 |

| 6 | + | 3 | = | 9 |

Plus means add, too.

We can read these **addition number sentences** like this:

6 starfish add 3 more starfish makes 9 starfish altogether.

3 starfish plus 6 more starfish equals 9 starfish in total.

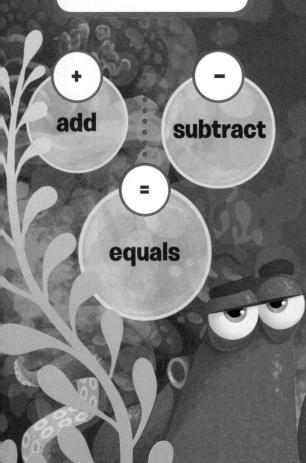

Equals =

The **equals** sign shows that a sum is balanced, so each side has the same answer.

$$2 + 3 = 4 + 1$$

Both sides of the sum equal 5.

Check your answers on pages 45 to 47.

What is subtraction? −

Sometimes subtraction means **taking away**.

Nemo counts 7 crabs. 4 crawl away. How many crabs are left?

$$7 - 4 = 3$$

Sometimes subtraction is **finding the difference** between two numbers.

Nemo counts 7 crabs and Dory counts 4 crabs. How many more crabs does Nemo count than Dory?

$$4 + 3 = 7$$

In **subtraction number sentences**, the larger number always goes first, like this:

$$7 - 4 = 3$$

Dory the blue tang fish grew up in a cosy coral home with her parents. The three fish were a happy family. There was just one problem: Dory struggled to remember things. To keep her safe, her parents taught her to say, "Hi, I'm Dory and I suffer from short-term memory loss."

One day, little Dory got lost in the great big ocean, alone. She couldn't remember where she had come from or how she had ended up there. Confused and scared she asked passing fish for help to get home, but they were unable to point her in the right direction. Dory kept on searching, but it wasn't long before she completely forgot what she was looking for.

Luckily, one day Dory bumped into a clownfish called Marlin. He was searching for his son, Nemo. Dory joined Marlin to find Nemo and when the adventure was over, the three fish settled happily on the Great Barrier Reef.

Let's Practise Numbers to 20

By now, you will know your numbers from 1 to 10, but do you know what comes next? The teen numbers sit between 10 and 20. They are made from a ten and ones. Count the number of bubbles each time, then write your answer in each box. Use the number line below to help. The first one has been done for you.

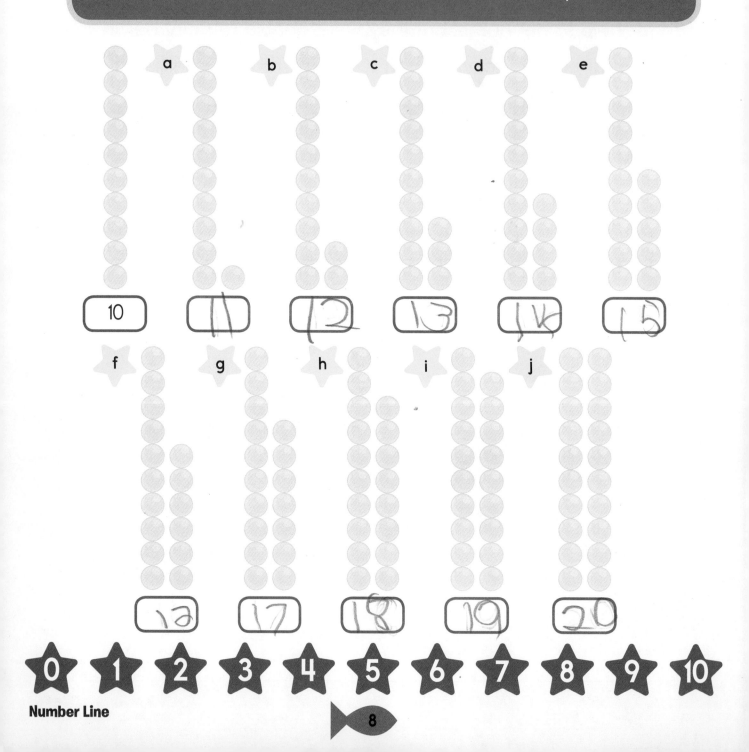

a b c d e

| 10 | 11 | 12 | 13 | 14 | 15 |

f g h i j

| 16 | 17 | 18 | 19 | 20 |

0 1 2 3 4 5 6 7 8 9 10

Number Line

8

Count the creatures, then write the total number in each box.

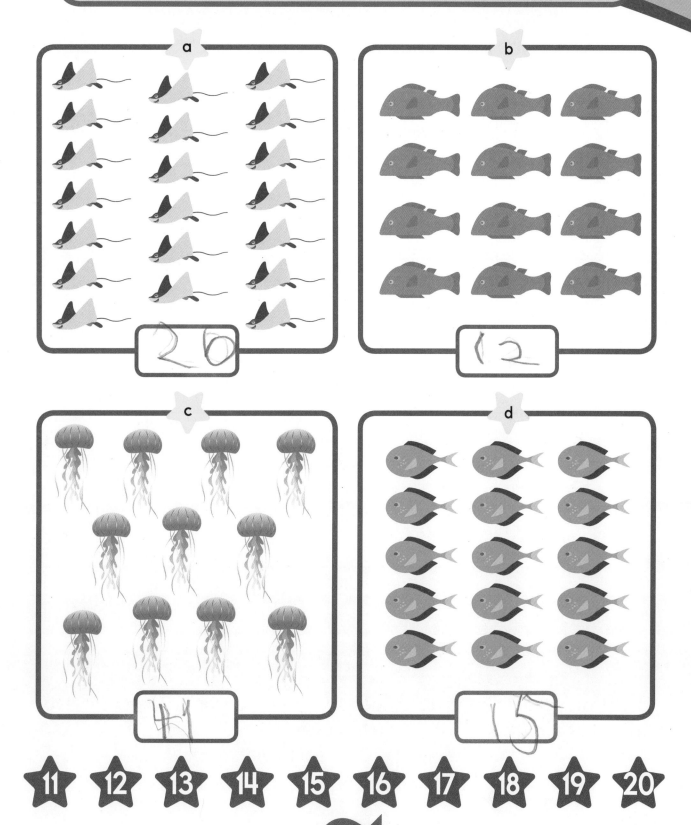

a

20

b

12

c

4

d

15

11 12 13 14 15 16 17 18 19 20

Let's Count to 100

Add the missing stickers to this 100 square.

1	2	3	4	5	6	7	8	9	10
11	12	13	14	15	16	17	18	19	20
21	22	23	24	25	26	27	28	29	30
31	32	33	34	35	36	37	38	39	40
41	42	43	44	45	46	47	48	49	50
51	52	53	54	55	56	57	58	59	60
61	62	63	64	65	66	67	68	69	70
71	72	73	74	75	76	77	78	79	80
81	82	83	84	85	86	87	88	89	90
91	92	93	94	95	96	97	98	99	100

Use the 100 square to count forwards and backwards. What number patterns do you notice in the different rows and columns?

Close your eyes, then put your finger on the 100 square. Open your eyes and say the number that is 1 more and the number that is 1 less. Try this a few times, saying the different numbers out loud.

Two-digit numbers are made from tens and ones.
Look at the pictures and write the numbers each time.
The first one has been done for you.

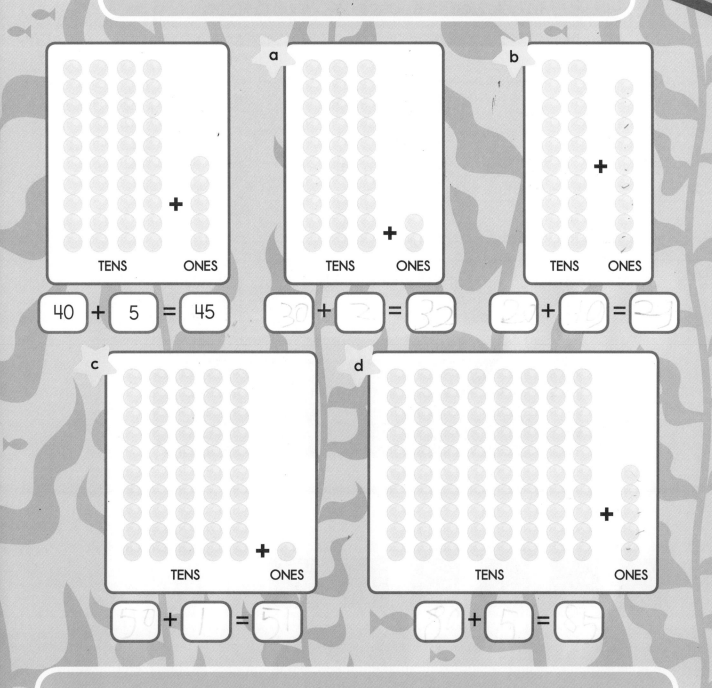

a

b

$40 + 5 = 45$

$30 + 2 = 32$

$20 + 10 = 20$

c

d

TENS   ONES

TENS   ONES

$50 + 1 = 51$

$80 + 5 = 85$

Now write the totals in order, from the smallest number to the largest:

20	32	45	51	85

smallest   **largest**

Let's Count in 2s, 5s and 10s

Use the pictures and the number line to help you to count in 2s. Write the totals.

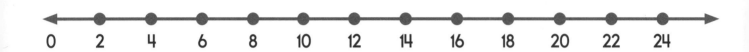

a  = 22 fish

b = 16 anchors

Use the pictures and the number line to help you to count in 5s. Write the totals.

c  = 30 dots

d = 45 shells

Use the pictures and the number line
to help you to count in 10s. Write the totals.

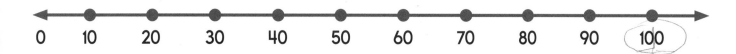

0   10   20   30   40   50   60   70   80   90   100

e   10p 10p 10p 10p 10p 10p 10p 10p 10p = 90 p

f   = 30 shells

g   = 5 0 bubbles

Look at these sequences.
Write in the missing numbers.

a	2	4	6	8	10	12	14	16
b	5	10	15	20	25	30	35	40
c	10	20	30	40	50	60	70	80

Let's Learn Number Facts to 9

Use the patterns to complete the number sentences.
First write pairs that total 5.

0	+	5	=	5

a

1	+	4	=	5

b

2	+	3	=	5

c

3	+	2	=	5

d

4	+	1	=	5

e

5	+	0	=	5

Now write pairs that total 8.

0	+	8	=	8

f

1	+	7	=	8

g

2	+	6	=	8

h

3	+	5	=	8

i

4	+	4	=	8

j

5	+	3	=	8

k

6	+	2	=	8

l

7	+	1	=	8

m

8	+	0	=	8

Find a piece of paper, and try to work out the pairs that total 6, 7 and 9.
You can find the answers on page 45.

Addition and subtraction are opposites in one relationship. Look at this picture.

5 → 5 is a **part**

8 is the **whole**
(or the **total**) ← 8

3 → 3 is a **part**

This shows us that:

5 + 3 = 8   8 - 5 = 3
3 + 5 = 8   8 - 3 = 5

Find the missing stickers to finish these addition and subtraction relationships.

a
8   2
     6

b
8   4
     4

c
7   2
     5

d
7   4
     3

e
9   6
     3

f
9   4
     5

Let's Learn Number Bonds to 10

Number bonds to 10 are two numbers that add together to make a total of 10. They are very useful to learn by heart.

If you know one addition fact, then you also know another one AND two subtraction facts!

I know this fact:

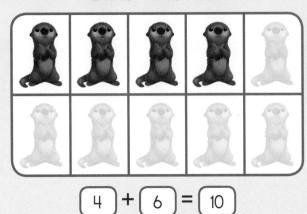

$4 + 6 = 10$

So know I know these facts:

$6 + 4 = 10$

$10 - 4 = 6$

$10 - 6 = 4$

Work out the missing number bond each time, then fill in the other addition and subtraction facts that it shows. Use the otter stickers to help you.

a

$5 + 5 = 10$

$5 + 5 = 10$

$10 - 5 = 5$

b

7 + 3 = 10

7 + 3 = 10

10 - 3 = 7

10 - 7 = 3

c

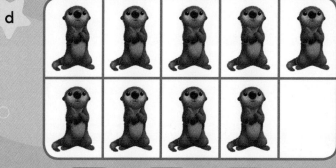

8 + 2 = 10

8 + 2 = 10

10 - 8 = 2

10 - 2 = 8

d

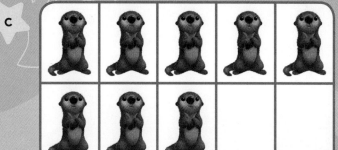

9 + 1 = 10

9 + 1 = 10

10 - 1 = 9

10 - 9 = 1

e

0 + 10 = 10

10 + 0 = 10

10 - 0 = 10

Dory, Marlin and Nemo were neighbours on the reef. They watched out for each other and when Nemo went to school, Dory sometimes went with him. One day, Dory joined Nemo's class on a school trip to see the stingray migration.

"Migration is about going home," the class teacher, Mr Ray, explained.

The word 'home' made Dory feel strange. Then one of the students asked her where she was from and she realised … she didn't know!

It was amazing watching the stingrays glide past. Mr Ray warned everyone about the undertow and something stirred inside Dory. She'd heard that before, too!

Dazzled by the sight, Dory drifted dangerously close to the rays and immediately found herself sucked into the current. A memory of her parents flashed into her mind before everything went black.

Let's Learn Number Bonds to 20

If you know your number bonds to 10,
then it is easy to work out the number bonds to 20.

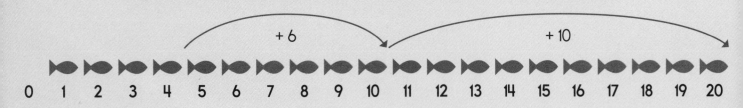

$+6$ $+10$

0 1 2 3 4 5 6 7 8 9 10 11 12 13 14 15 16 17 18 19 20

4 + 6 = 10   and   4 + 16 = 20

Use the number line to help you with these sums:

0 1 2 3 4 5 6 7 8 9 10 11 12 13 14 15 16 17 18 19 20

a   3 + 7 = 10   and   3 + 17 = 20

b   5 + 5 = 10   and   5 + 15 = 20

c   6 + 4 = 10   and   16 + 4 = 20

d   7 + 3 = 10   and   17 + 3 = 20

20

Now try these subtractions. Use your number bond facts first, then the number line if you get stuck.

0 1 2 3 4 5 6 7 8 9 10 11 12 13 14 15 16 17 18 19 20

a   10 − 2 = 8   so   20 − 2 = 18

b   10 − 3 = 7   so   20 − 13 = 7

c   10 − 1 = 9   so   20 − 19 = 1

d   10 − 4 = 6   so   20 − 6 = 14

e   10 − 5 = 5   so   20 − 5 = 15

Let's Find Doubles and Halves

Doubles and halves are the opposites of each other. If you know that double 3 is 6, then you also know that half of 6 is 3.

Use the picture example to help you write a sum to double these numbers.

3 + 3 = 6

a

4 + 4 = 8

b

5 + 5 = 10

c

d

e

7 + 7 = 14   8 + 8 = 16   10 + 10 = 20

Use the picture example to help you halve these numbers and complete the number sentences.

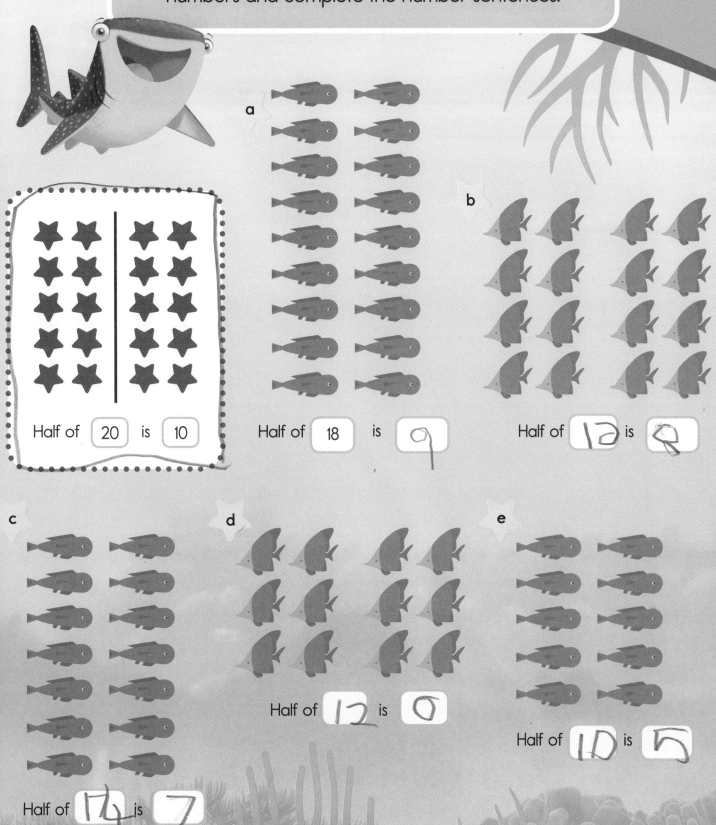

Half of 20 is 10

a

Half of 18 is 9

b

Half of 12 is 8

c

Half of 14 is 7

d

Half of 12 is 0

e

Half of 10 is 5

Let's Multiply and Divide

These pictures help to show the links between multiplication and division. We use the words **lots of** and **groups of**.

This picture shows that 6 groups of 2 are equal to 2 groups of 6.

Look at the pictures below. Write the totals in the boxes.

c

a

b

☐ anchors

☐ fish

☐ seaweed plants

d There are 3 fish tanks. Stick 4 fish stickers in each tank. How many fish are there altogether? ☐ fish

a Dory has 18 seaweed plants. She shares them equally between herself, Marlin and Nemo. Put in the stickers, then count how many plants each fish gets.

6

6

6

plants   plants   plants

b Dory has 8 pearls. She shares them equally between Nemo and Marlin. Add stickers to show how many pearls they each get.

pearls   pearls

25

Let's Practise Fractions

When we find a fraction of a whole shape
or quantity, we need to split it into equal parts.

a

To show $\frac{1}{2}$, we need to split the whole into 2 equal parts.
Tick the shapes where the colour part is equal to half.

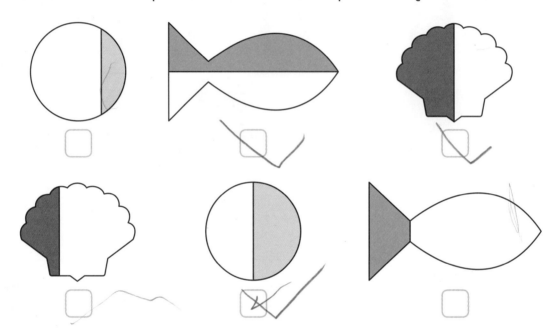

To show $\frac{1}{4}$, we need to split the whole into 4 equal parts.

b Colour $\frac{1}{2}$ of each shape blue and another $\frac{1}{4}$ of each shape red.

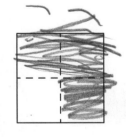 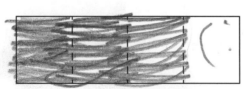  

Dory's friends are going to share the picnic plants below. Find the same stickers from the sticker sheet and share the food out fairly between Pearl, Nemo, Tad and Sheldon.

Pearl

Nemo

Tad

Sheldon

When she awoke, Dory tried to recall the memory she'd had before she blacked out. Then Nemo said he had heard her murmur, "The Jewel of Morro Bay, California."

Memories flooded Dory's mind. "My family!" she exclaimed. "I remember my family!"

Suddenly, Dory swam off to find her parents, leaving Marlin and Nemo no choice but to follow.

"Hey!" Nemo called. "Wait!"

"Dory, California's all the way across the ocean," said Marlin.

Dory stopped at the edge of the reef and stared out at the great ocean beyond. It seemed to go on forever.

Dory felt sad. Now that she remembered her family, she missed them. "Do you know what that feels like?" she asked Marlin. Marlin knew better than anyone what it felt like to be separated from family. He had missed Nemo every second that they were apart. "Yes, I know what that feels like," he sighed.

Nemo was sure his dad could help Dory find her parents. "You can get us all the way across the ocean, right?" he asked. "No," said Marlin. "But I know a guy who can."

It wouldn't be easy, but the friends were about to begin a new adventure together. They would ride the California current.

Let's Use Money

Every coin has a different value.

1p 2p 5p 10p 20p 50p

Dory and Nemo have found some treasure! Add up the coins in each treasure chest and then write the total in each box. Try counting in multiples of 2, 5 and 10 to make it quicker.

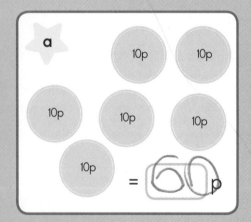

a

10p 10p
10p 10p 10p
10p

= 60 p

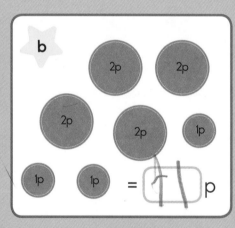

b

2p 2p
2p 2p 1p
1p 1p

= 11 p

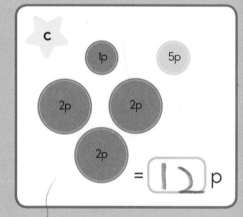

c

1p 5p
2p 2p
2p

= 12 p

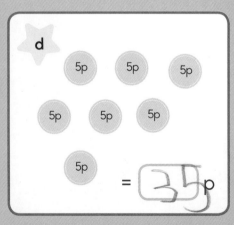

d

5p 5p 5p
5p 5p 5p
5p

= 35 p

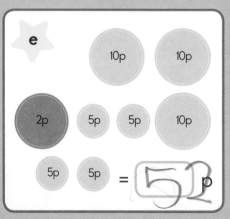

e

10p 10p
2p 5p 5p 10p
5p 5p

= 52 p

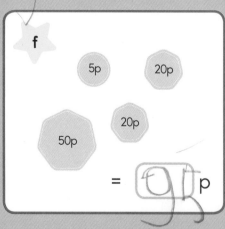

f

5p 20p
20p
50p

= 95 p

Time to go shopping! On this page, cross out the money that is spent. Now count up the coins to work out how much money is left.

a You have 20p. You spend 6p. How much money do you have left?

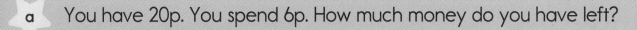

2p 2p 2p 2p 2p 2p 2p 2p 2p 2p = 20 p

b You have 80p. You spend 30p. How much money do you have left?

10p 10p 10p 10p 10p 10p 10p 10p = 80 p

c You have 55p. You spend 20p. How much money do you have left?

5p 5p 5p 5p 5p 5p 5p 5p 5p 5p 5p = 55 p

d Your friend spends 19p. Draw the coins she could use to make 19p. Think of three different ways, using as few coins as possible.

Let's Tell the Time

Let's learn to tell the time to the nearest hour and half hour. Complete the sentences below using the time shown on each clock.

hour hand

There are 60 minutes in an hour. This clock shows half past 12, which means it is half an hour, or 30 minutes, after 12 o'clock.

minute hand

a

I wake up at

....

b

I eat breakfast at

....

c

I start school at

....

d

I have playtime at

....

e

I have lunch at

....

f

I go home at

....

g

I go to sleep at

....

Draw the hands on the clocks to show the time when these things happen. Use a ruler and remember to draw the hour hand shorter than the minute hand.

a

School starts at half past 8.

b

The class has a snack at 11 o'clock.

c

The class has lunch at 1 o'clock.

d

Everyone plays hide-and-seek at half past 2.

e

At home, storytime is at 6 o'clock.

f

Bedtime is at half past 7.

Remember!

When the long hand points straight up at the 12, the time is something o'clock.

Hooray, you've finished! Add an otter sticker here.

Let's Look at Shapes

Look at these 2D shapes. How many sides and corners do they have? Are the sides curved or straight?

rectangle　　　**square**　　　**circle**　　　**triangle**

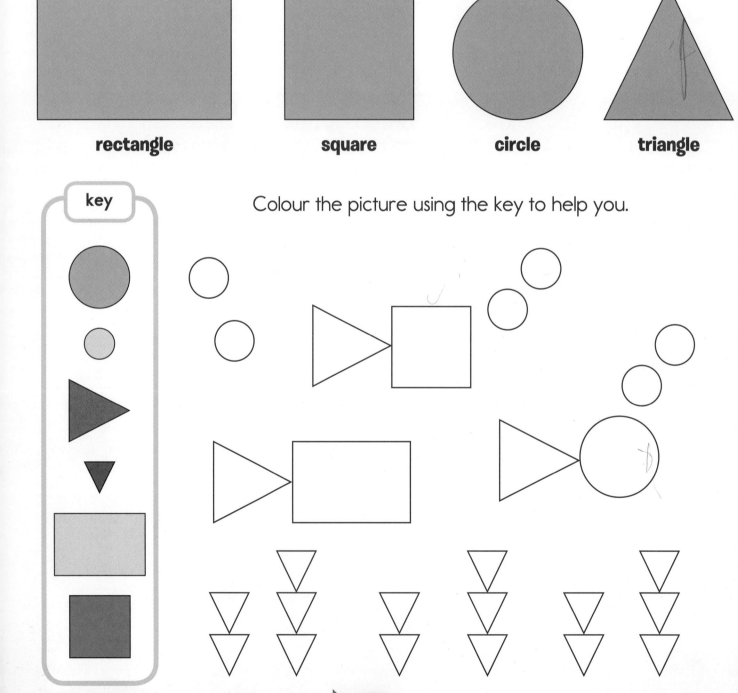

key

Colour the picture using the key to help you.

Here are some 3D shapes.
They have edges, faces and corners.

corner

face

edge

pyramid　　　　　　**cube**　　　　　　**cuboid**

Read the clues to work out which shape is being described.
Write the name of the shape and add the right sticker each time.

a   I am a 3D shape. I have a square base and 4 triangular faces.

b   I am a 2D shape. I have 1 edge, no straight sides and no corners.

c   I am a 3D shape. I have 6 identical faces. Each face is a square.

....

d   I am a 2D shape. I have 4 corners and 2 pairs of equal sides – but they are not all equal.

....

Let's Practise Measurement

Under the sea, things come in many different shapes and sizes!

Hank

Destiny

Cross out the word that is wrong in each sentence.

- Hank is bigger / smaller than Destiny.
- Destiny is bigger / smaller than Hank.

Circle the seaweed plant that is shorter.

Now draw some seaweed that is shorter than both.

How many shells long are each of the friends?

a

☐ shells

b

☐ shells

We use the word **capacity** to describe the amount of liquid there is. The words **mass** or **weight** describe how heavy or light an object is.

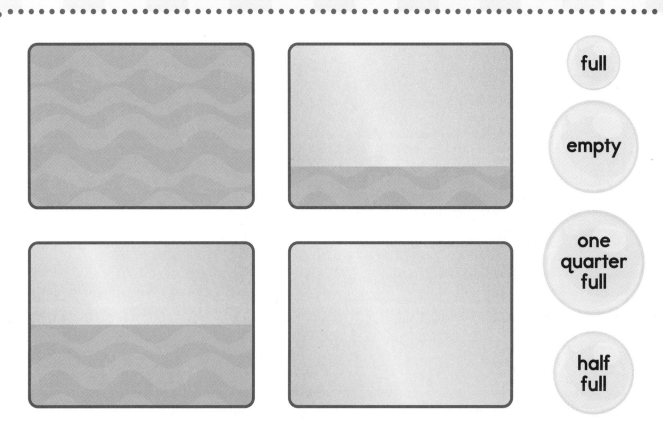

full

empty

one quarter full

half full

Look at the amount of liquid in each of these fish tanks. Draw a line to match each fish tank to the right description.

Look at this see-saw.

Put a tick next to the crab that is heavier.

Put a cross next to the crab that is lighter.

Let's Make a *Finding Dory* Game

Play this fun game with your family or friends.
Who will be the first to find Dory?

You will need:

- the counter stickers from the sticker sheet
- a small piece of card
- scissors
- a dice
- 2 to 4 players

Make your counters by sticking the counter stickers onto a piece of card. Cut them out carefully.

Scissors are sharp. Ask a grown-up to help you.

Marlin

Destiny

Bailey

Hank

How to play:

1. Each player should choose a counter and place it on the START space.

2. The youngest player goes first.

3. When it is their turn, each player rolls the dice, and adds up the dots to see how many spaces to move along the board.

4. Try to say the number that you land on out loud.

5. If you land at the bottom of some seaweed, move your counter to the top of it. If you land at the top of a pipe, slide your counter down to the bottom of the pipe.

6. The winner is the first player to reach the FINISH space.

100	99	98	97	96	95	94	93	92	91
81	82	83	84	85	86	87	88	89	90
80	79	78	77	76	75	74	73	72	71
61	62	63	64	65	66	67	68	69	70
60	59	58	57	56	55	54	53	52	51
41	42	43	44	45	46	47	48	49	50
40	39	38	37	36	35	34	33	32	31
21	22	23	24	25	26	27	28	29	30
20	19	18	17	16	15	14	13	12	11
1	2	3	4	5	6	7	8	9	10

START

Here Are All the Things I Can Do

Put a fish sticker next to all of the things that you can do!

I can ...

understand the +, – and = signs

say one more or one less in numbers to 100

read and write the numbers 1 to 20 in numerals

count in 2s, 5s and 10s

read and write the numbers to 100 in numerals

solve addition and subtraction sums

say how many tens and ones are in a 2-digit number

say number bonds to 10 and 20

order a set of 2-digit numbers by size

solve missing number problems

work out doubles
to 10

solve problems
involving money

work out half of even
numbers to 20

tell the time to the
nearest hour and
half past the hour

solve multiplication
and division problems

recognise and
name some 2D
and 3D shapes

find $\frac{1}{2}$ and $\frac{1}{4}$
of shapes and
small quantities

compare different
lengths, weights
and quantities

More Activities to Share with Your Child

Practise maths every day

Maths is an essential skill that we use in practical ways every day when we cook, shop, play and much, much more. Be positive about maths with your child, as children are quick to pick up on negative vibes that parents may give off if they didn't enjoy maths at school.

Go on a number hunt

Numbers are everywhere! Children should be encouraged to recognise and read numbers around them. This will help them to understand that numbers have different purposes. You might spot the number 64 bus or house number 98. Look for numbers written as prices in shops. Count the number of red cars you can see on a journey or the number of peas on your plate.

Learn to speak maths!

Help children to develop their comparative language by using words such as shorter, longer, taller, lighter, heavier, more, less, fewer, most or least. Make observations such as, "The egg is lighter than the apple. The apple is heavier than the egg," or, "I have the most counters. My friend has fewer counters than me."

Understanding time

Time is a tricky concept for young children, but it is easy to bring into everyday life. Talk about what day of the week and month of the year it is and help them to learn the weeks and months in order. Ask questions like, "What day was it yesterday? What day will it be tomorrow? In which month is your birthday?" Help children to identify what times of day and on which days of the week they do certain activities: "What time do you get up in the morning? On which days do you go to school?"

Using coins

Ask your child to sort a mixture of coins and try adding two coins together to find the total. Practise counting in multiples of 2s, 5s and 10s with 2p, 5p and 10p coins. You could ask questions like, "Show me 6p. If I give you 4p more, how much money will you have?" or "I have 15p and the pencil costs 20p. How much more money do I need?" See how many different ways your child can make the target number with coins. Make it real by allowing your child to pay for small-value items using coins and count out any change. Children can find it hard to understand how one 5p coin is of equal value to five 1p coins. In this case, use counters or blocks to make the numbers.

Fluency with mental maths facts

Use journeys to practise mental maths. Say a number and ask your child to tell you a number that is one more or two more, one less or two less. Say two or three single-digit numbers out loud (for example, 3, 1 and 4) and ask your child to tell you the total.

Play number 'ping pong' with doubling and halving facts or number bonds to 10 or 20. To practise doubling, you say, "6" and your child pings back, "12." To practise halving, you say, "18" and your child pings back, "9."

More Activities to Share with Your Child

Make a tens frame

Cut 2 cups from a 12-egg carton so that you are left with a box with 10 cups. Use 2 different colours of buttons or other small objects to count and add. Ask your child to put 5 objects of one colour in the box, in separate cups, and then add 3 more of a different colour in the empty cups. See if your child can quickly look at the box to estimate how many objects there are altogether, without counting them all. Then count the objects together to check. You can also find pairs of numbers that total 10 this way. Make another 10-cup box to find the pairs that total 20.

Understanding 2-digit numbers

As children become confident using numbers up to 100, it is important that they understand the value of these numbers. Practical resources like using bundles of 10 straws, sets of tens frames and sticks of 10 building blocks are excellent for helping children understand that our number system is based on units of 1, 10, and so on. For example, the number 56 is made up of 5 units of 10, which are worth 50, and 6 units of 1, which are worth 6. Children need to practise partitioning and re-combining 2-digit numbers: "I partition 73 into 70 and 3. I re-combine 70 and 3 to make 73."

Maths at mealtimes

Food is an excellent way of making maths fun. Your child could practise weighing and measuring skills by helping you to follow recipes. Try counting out and comparing different quantities. Food is a great way to develop tricky concepts like sharing, dividing and using fractions. You could ask your child to share out a bunch of 12 grapes between 4 people, for example, or to describe what a quarter of a cake would look like.

Page 8

a) 11   b) 12   c) 13   d 14

e) 15   f) 16   g) 17   h) 18

i) 19   j) 20

Page 9

a) 20   b) 12   c) 11   d) 15

Page 10

1	2	3	4	5	6	7	8	9	10
11	12	13	14	15	16	17	18	19	20
21	22	23	24	25	26	27	28	29	30
31	32	33	34	35	36	37	38	39	40
41	42	43	44	45	46	47	48	49	50
51	52	53	54	55	56	57	58	59	60
61	62	63	64	65	66	67	68	69	70
71	72	73	74	75	76	77	78	79	80
81	82	83	84	85	86	87	88	89	90
91	92	93	94	95	96	97	98	99	100

Page 11

a) 30 + 2 = 32   b) 20 + 9 = 29

c) 50 + 1 = 51   d) 80 + 5 = 85

29	32	45	51	85

Pages 12–13

a) 22 fish   b) 16 anchors   c) 30 dots

d) 45 shells   e) 90p   f) 30 shells

g) 50 bubbles

a)

2	4	6	8	10	12	14	16

b)

5	10	15	20	25	30	35	40

c)

10	20	30	40	50	60	70	80

Page 14

a) 1 + 4 = 5   b) 2 + 3 = 5   c) 3 + 2 = 5

d) 4 + 1 = 5   e) 5 + 0 = 5

f) 1 + 7 = 8   g) 2 + 6 = 8   h) 3 + 5 = 8

i) 4 + 4 = 8   j) 5 + 3 = 8   k) 6 + 2 = 8

l) 7 + 1 = 8   m) 8 + 0 = 8

Pairs that total 6:

0 + 6 = 6   1 + 5 = 6   2 + 4 = 6

3 + 3 = 6   4 + 2 = 6   5 + 1 = 6

6 + 0 = 6

Answers

Pairs that total 7:

0 + 7 = 7   1 + 6 = 7   2 + 5 = 7

3 + 4 = 7   4 + 3 = 7   5 + 2 = 7

6 + 1 = 7   7 + 0 = 7

Pairs that total 9:

0 + 9 = 9   1 + 8 = 9   2 + 7 = 9

3 + 6 = 9   4 + 5 = 9   5 + 4 = 9

6 + 3 = 9   7 + 2 = 9   8 + 1 = 9

9 + 0 = 9

Page 15

a) 8 → 2, 6

b) 8 → 4, 4

c) 7 → 2, 5

d) 7 → 4, 3

e) 9 → 6, 3

f) 9 → 4, 5

Pages 16–17

a) 5 + 5 = 10
   5 + 5 = 10
   10 − 5 = 5

b) 7 + 3 = 10
   3 + 7 = 10
   10 − 7 = 3
   10 − 3 = 7

c) 8 + 2 = 10
   2 + 8 = 10
   10 − 8 = 2
   10 − 2 = 8

d) 9 + 1 = 10
   1 + 9 = 10
   10 − 9 = 1
   10 − 1 = 9

e) 10 + 0 = 10
   0 + 10 = 10
   10 − 0 = 10

Page 20

a) 3 + 7 = 10   and   3 + 17 = 20

b) 5 + 5 = 10   and   5 + 15 = 20

c) 6 + 4 = 10   and   16 + 4 = 20

d) 7 + 3 = 10   and   17 + 3 = 20

Page 21

a) 10 − 2 = 8   so   20 − 2 = 18

b) 10 − 3 = 7   so   20 − 13 = 7

c) 10 − 1 = 9   so   20 − 19 = 1

d) 10 − 4 = 6   so   20 − 6 = 14

e) 10 − 5 = 5   so   20 − 5 = 15

Page 22

a) 4 + 4 = 8   b) 5 + 5 = 10

c) 7 + 7 = 14   d) 8 + 8 = 16

e) 10 + 10 = 20

Page 23

a) Half of 18 is 9   b) Half of 16 is 8

c) Half of 14 is 7   d) Half of 12 is 6

e) Half of 10 is 5

Page 24

a) 4 anchors   b) 12 fish

c) 15 seaweed plants   d) 12 fish

Page 25

a)

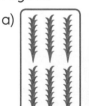

Dory, Marlin and Nemo each have 6 seaweed plants.

b)

Marlin and Nemo each have 4 pearls.

Page 26

Page 27

Each friend has:

Page 30

a) 60p   b) 11p   c) 12p

d) 35p   e) 52p   f) 95p

Page 31

a) 14p   b) 50p   c) 35p

d)

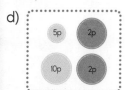

Page 32

a) I wake up at 7 o'clock.

b) I eat breakfast at half past 7.

c) I start school at 9 o'clock.

d) I have playtime at half past 10.

e) I have lunch at 12 o'clock.

f) I go home at half past 3.

g) I go to sleep at 8 o'clock.

Page 33

a)   b)   c)

d)   e)   f)

Page 35

a)   b)   c)   d)

pyramid   circle   cube   rectangle

Page 36

Hank is ~~bigger~~ / smaller than Destiny.

Destiny is bigger / ~~smaller~~ than Hank.

a) 6 shells   b) 3 shells

Page 37

full   one quarter full   half full   empty

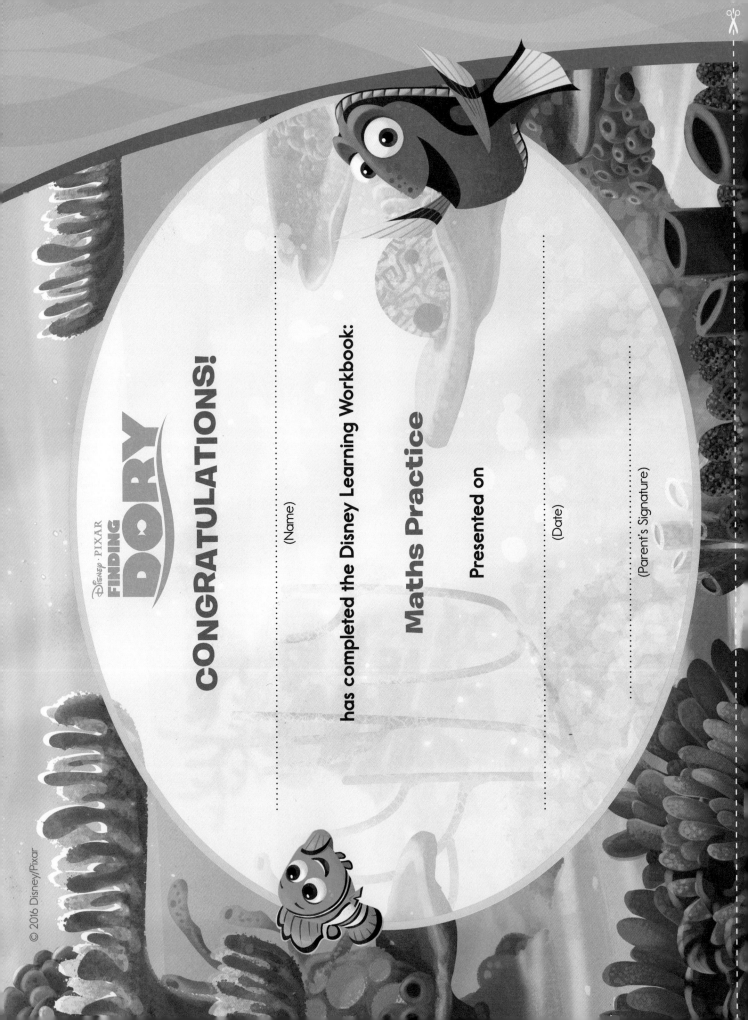

Disney · PIXAR

FINDING DORY

CONGRATULATIONS!

....

(Name)

has completed the Disney Learning Workbook:

Maths Practice

Presented on

....

(Date)

....

(Parent's Signature)